C000293045

Cover illustration: A posed photograph of Boer riflemen sheltering behind a railway embankment. The two men lying prone have Martini rifles.

1. Boer riflemen in a shallow trench, showing a typical assortment of dress, including (extreme right) a coloured sports blazer and a straw boater. The man fourth from right has a clip of bullets ready for insertion in his magazine rifle.

The Boer War

P. J. HAYTHORNTHWAITE

ARMS AND ARMOUR PRESS

Published in South Africa by
MEDIA HOUSE PUBLICATIONS (PTY) LTD

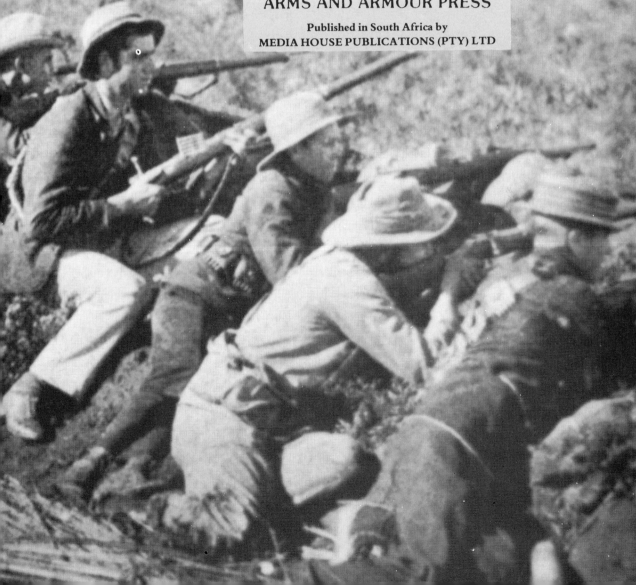

Introduction

irst published in Great Britain in 1987 by Arms and
rmour Press Ltd., Link House, West Street, Poole,
orset BH15 1LL.

istributed in the USA by Sterling Publishing Co.
c., 2 Park Avenue, New York, NY 10016.

istributed in Australia by
apricorn Link (Australia) Pty. Ltd., P.O. Box 665,
ane Cove, New South Wales 2066.

ritish Library Cataloguing in Publication data:
aythornthwaite, Philip J.
he Boer war.
. Uniforms, Military   2. South African
'ar, 1899–1902
. Title
55.1'4'0968   UC480

BN 0-85368-764-1

dited and designed by Roger Chesneau; typeset by
ypesetters (Birmingham) Ltd., printed and bound
. Great Britain by The Bath Press, Avon.

Though contemporary photographs are the most valuable source of information about the uniforms and equipment worn during the Boer War, a number of points must be borne in mind. First, certain 'active service' photographs (especially some published at the time in such works as the *Navy & Army Illustrated*, *With the Flag to Pretoria* and *After Pretoria: The Guerilla War* – all of which have been used as sources for some of the photographs in this collection) are obviously 'posed' and frequently misleadingly captioned. Even more misleading is the deliberate alteration of photographs before publication, to turn a commonplace image into one which purports to originate from the field of battle. Whilst a number of 'studio' portraits are included in the following pages, the emphasis has been placed upon those taken in the field; as in every campaign, the latter are evidence of the often wide divergence between the uniforms which should have been worn and those which were actually worn, adapted by virtue of personal preference or the wear and tear of campaigning.

The British Army embarked on the campaign wearing a uniform consisting of a khaki tunic and trousers, with puttees and sun helmet, khaki having been made the universal service uniform in 1896. The original khaki drill material was found to be insufficiently warm and was replaced by serge, the pattern remaining unchanged. The most obvious alteration was in the head-dress, the helmet being found less practical than the felt slouch hat favoured by colonial units; such hats became the popular style throughout the British forces.

The very composition of the Boer forces – civilians formed into *ad hoc* units to exploit their peculiar skills of bushcraft, marksmanship and mobility – precluded the adoption of conventional uniforms, and their means of identification was often restricted to a coloured cockade or hat-band. Equipment was similarly varied, and, contrary to popular belief, their weapons were not exclusively the Mauser rifle but included an increasing use of captured British *matériel* as the war progressed. The only uniforms worn in Boer service were those of their regular troops, the *Staatsartillerie* of the Transvaal (South African Republic, or ZAR) and the Orange Free State (OVS), and those worn by some of the foreign volunteers from Europe and America.

A feature of the Boer War was the involvement of civilian-soldiers; virtually the entire Boer forces were irregular soldiers, and a large proportion of the British forces were volunteers or yeomen from Britain and her overseas territories, including Australia, New Zealand, Canada and even India and Ceylon. A significant contribution was made by the Imperial Yeomanry, active-service squadrons formed from the British home-defence force, which, like the Mounted Infantry, were a method of combating the highly mobile Boer guerrillas; though uniformed similarly to the regulars, their presence extended the use of the slouch hat and similar practical features.

The author extends his gratitude to all those who assisted with this book, particularly to Andrew May and Kevin R. Young, and especially to H. V. Wilkinson for his help in tracing some of the rarer contemporary sources. As usual, any errors or omissions are the author's responsibility entirely.

Philip J. Haythornthwaite

◀2
. A trumpeter of the Royal Scots Greys, in South
\frican kit. Note the spare boots carried at the front
>f the saddle, the net of forage, and the presence of
oth a bugle and a long cavalry trumpet.

▲3

▲4

3, 4. The overseas service uniform of the British Army. These men, of the Warwickshire Regiment, wear the khaki tunic or 'frock', trousers and puttees, and a khaki helmet with a pagri, the last a cloth strip 4in wide and sometimes 24ft long. The 1888-pattern (Slade-Wallace) equipment, stained khaki-brown on service,

includes ammunition pouches, haversack, canteen and rolled blanket, with the valise omitted in this case.

5. Officers of the 16th Lancers. Note their highly polished gauntlets and leggings, and the steel shoulder-chains worn by cavalry regiments.

▼5

6▲   7▲

6. Pattern of khaki drill or serge 'frock', authorized July 1897, 'fitted loosely to admit warm clothing being worn underneath if necessary'. It had pointed cuffs, brass buttons, stand-and-fall collar and patch pockets; cavalry and Royal Horse Artillery wore chains instead of shoulder-straps.

7. The 'frock' worn by Scottish regiments, made to resemble a doublet; the pockets had two buttons covered in khaki cloth, the front corners were rounded, and its cuffs were of 'gauntlet' style.

8. A. The tropical helmet, pattern of June 1898. It was made of khaki cloth on cork, or white with a khaki cover, and *Dress Regulations* noted that 'Officers should be careful that their

Tradesmen do not supply them with "smart" looking helmets instead of those capable of affording protection from the sun'. A khaki havelock or neck-curtain could be worn 'when the severity of the climate necessitates it', and regimental insignia were often worn on the side. **B.** An alternative pattern worn by officers was the 'Wolseley' helmet, authorized in September 1899 officially for the West African and Chinese Regiments but worn extensively in South Africa and officially replacing the previous pattern in 1904. **C.** The 'pith hat', an alternative permitted by *Dress Regulations*: 'Pith, covered with khaki, brim about 3½ inches in width, khaki-covered zinc ventilator at the top, green lining'.

8▼

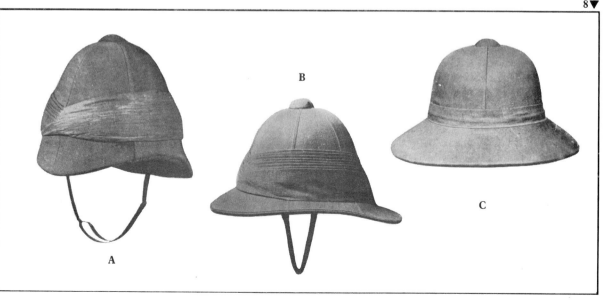

B

A   C

9. Lt.Col. Frederick W. Kitchener, brevet Brigadier-General (1900). Brother of Lord Kitchener, he wears the uniform of his West Yorkshire Regiment, illustrating a typical helmet flash – the woven title cut from the red shoulder-strap of the home service tunic, stitched to the pagri or helmet-cover, usually on a red square (though varieties existed).

10. Officers of the 1st Battalion, Royal Irish Fusiliers. 'Wolseley' helmets are worn here with typical officers' dress, including the brown leather 'Sam Browne' belt, here with double shoulder-braces instead of the single diagonal brace over the right shoulder.

11. Brigadier-General Thomas Cole Porter, commanding the 1st Cavalry Brigade, 1899–1900. His 'Sam Browne' has shoulder braces, and the pistol a lanyard around his neck; the sword is probably the regimental pattern of his unit, the 6th Dragoon Guards.

12. 'C' Squadron, Royal Scots Greys. Helmet flashes were not popular with the cavalry, though some used the letters from their red shoulder-strap (e.g. the Royal Dragoons, '1RD'); others used coloured pagris, like the Royal Scots Greys, theirs either red stripes on white or with a red strip twisted through them.

◀9

13. A sergeant of the Mounted Infantry with full field equipment. Unlike the cavalry, who were armed with shorter carbines, he carries the full-length 1895 Lee-Enfield magazine rifle, but he wears cavalry boots instead of the infantry puttees. The horse furniture is that used by the cavalry.

14. Gordon Highlanders using a church as a storehouse at

Ladysmith. It is interesting to note that the sporran is still in use, even on active service, despite its serving little purpose.

15. Officers of the Royal Irish Rifles – a typical group in service uniform, posed in a railway siding with a truck in the background. Note how many carry rifles in addition to their pistols, and the varied manner in which their equipment is worn.

▲16 ▼17

▼18

16. Examples of Boer uniforms, as worn by NCOs of the Johannesburg Volunteers, a corps which had served against the Swazis. Disbanded before hostilities but subsequently re-formed, its 200 cavalry and 800 infantry were organized in 'national' companies, one of 'Hollanders' (Boers), one German, one 'Latin' (French, Spanish and Italian), and a 'mixed' company including British, Russians and Scandinavians. Its officers included the British Major B. A. Hall, late Bechuanaland Police; Major L. E. Van Diggelen, late Dutch Navy; Major Kropp, a Hanoverian Crimea veteran; and Lt. Rossiger, one of the few survivors of 'Hicks Pasha's' army. Note the *fanions* (pennants) carried on rifles in the French style.

17. Major P. E. Erasmus. The ZAR *Staatsartillerie* wore a vaguely Dutch-style full dress, comprising a white helmet with white plume, a dark blue tunic and trousers with black facings and braid, with a black pouch-belt with whistle and chain, stars on the collar and stripes on the cuff for officers. The horse battery had low busbies with upright plumes.

18. Commandant Pietrus Jacobus Joubert (1831–1900), commandant-general of the Boer armies 1899–1900. He was a veteran of the Kaffir wars, and upon his death Lord Roberts sent Kruger a note of condolence, saying of Joubert: 'His personal gallantry was only surpassed by his humane conduct and chivalrous bearing'. In this photograph he wears a European-style patrol jacket.

19. The British commander 'Bobs', Earl Roberts of Kandahar (1832–1914), in service dress, including a somewhat oversize cap.

20. Earl Kitchener of Khartoum (1850–1916) as a major-general, wearing field service uniform, 1898, with the new 'Wolseley' helmet which made its appearance in the Sudan.

19▼

20▼

21. Lt. Gen. Sir John French, photographed Middleburg, wearing staff uniform. He was later Earl of Ypres and commander of the British Expeditionary Force, 1914–15.
22. Breakfast at Ladysmith, before provisions ran short. This is a good illustration of camp equipment including mess-tins and camp kettle, bottles and jars made from shells, and 'undress' uniform.
23. The 42nd Field Battery, Royal Artillery, sent to South Africa from Bombay. This photograph shows the ordinary working dress of the British soldier – shirt and trousers, with jacket removed.
24. Regimental variations on the ordinary uniform. Lieutenant and Adjutant T. G. Matheson, 1st Bn. Coldstream Guards, wears the regimental tunic with its buttons in pairs (the spacing being the traditional method distinguishing the five Guards regiments), with the red feather hackle and Garter star badge in the hat.
◀21

22▲   23▼   24▼

25. Infantry stretcher-bearers evacuating casualties or collecting the dead. Note the use of neck-shades attached to the helmets.
26. Cooks of the Cameronians (Scottish Rifles) in camp at Springfield, showing an assortment of headgear, including slouch hats and a civilian hat (right).
27. Lt. Gen. Sir H. M. Leslie Rundle, commander of the 8th Division, South African Field Force. Kitchener's chief of staff in the Sudan and advisor at Omdurman, Sir Leslie Rundle was an Ulundi veteran who achieved the temporary rank of Lieutenant-General at the remarkably early age of 43. He is shown here wearing ordinary khaki service uniform with the 'Wolseley' helmet, a 'Sam Browne' belt with single brace, non-regulation gauntlets and, apparently, a Royal Artillery sword.

28. Lt. Gen. the Hon.
Neville G. Lyttleton. A
veteran of 35 years'
service, much of it in the
Rifle Brigade, Neville
Lyttleton was appointed
to command the 4th
Division after service at
Spion Kop. Here he
wears the khaki service
uniform with its scarlet
gorget patches, showing
the design of the pointed
cuff to good effect. His
leather equipment is
worn with the double
shoulder-braces, the
alternative method to the
diagonal shoulder-strap.
29. Jack and Jokey:
scouts of the 2nd Bn.
West Yorkshire
Regiment, 1902.
30. Hairdressing in the
field: a barber photo-
graphed at work in a
British 'flying column'.
Owing to the climate, it
was common for the
tunic to be removed and
the men to perform their
duties in shirt-sleeves
during the daytime.
31. An officer of the
Rifle Brigade shaving in
the open air. A typical
field kit, comprising
rolled mattress, hair-
brushes, shaving-mirror
and a Gladstone bag to
hold it, is shown. The
chair was probably
'borrowed' from a Boer
household.

◀28

29 ▲

30▲ 31▼

▲32   ▼33

34▲

2. The regimental shoemaker of the Border Regiment working
inside a wrecked truck from the armoured train ambushed near
Chieveley; note the 'SB' brassard of the stretcher-bearer (centre).
3. Maxim gun and supporting infantry. Note the box-shaped, felt-
covered metal canteen worn by the figure on the right instead of the
oval canteen of the 1888 valise equipment. Mess tins are worn at the
rear of the belts.
4. Tea on the veldt. Kitchener complained that the guerrillas
would never be caught whilst British officers marched with 'kitchen
ranges, pianos and harmoniums', not greatly exaggerated as these
photographs demonstrate. The officers' mess of the East Yorkshire
Regiment, with mess-waggon, is seen in the background. The
standing figure on the left has turned his helmet back to front to
provide a better eye-shade.
35. The 2nd Battalion, the West Yorkshire Regiment, en route from
Wakerstroom to Volksrust in the month following the cessation of
hostilities, June 1902. This previously unpublished photograph
shows a 'Wolseley' helmet bearing the regimental striped pagri flash.

35▼

▲36 ▼37

38▲ 39▼

40▲

36. A halt on the march: an officers' camp of the 6th Dragoon Guards of French's cavalry division, showing General Brabazon (centre, with cane). The regiment's horses are in lines in the background. Note the officer seated on the left, dining off a packing case; his helmet is worn back to front, to use the neck-shade as a peak.

37. Officers of the 2nd Bn. the Devonshire Regiment along the Tugela River. Note the wide variety of dress, including a woollen sweater and (extreme right) white tennis shoes. The medical officer's red cross brassard shows clearly in the fading light.

38. Lt. Col. (later Field Marshal) Sir H. S. Rawlinson, Bart., Coldstream Guards, seen in a photograph dated February 1901. The illustration shows the scarlet gorget patches of Staff appointment, and the usual practice of wearing the medal ribbons on a detachable bar, not as a set stitched to each tunic.

39. Lt. Gen. Sir Ian Hamilton, photographed when commanding the Mounted Infantry, just before his pursuit of De Wet. The MI bodyguard is considerably less tidily attired than his general!

40. Lt. Col. G. F. Gorringe, ADC to Chief of Staff, 1899–1900; he took command of a flying column nicknamed 'Gorringe's Light Oxen'. The New Zealand-style hat was the pattern selected by Baden Powell for use by his scouting movement.

▲41

▲42　▼43

41. An infantry skirmish-line, reputedly at Ladysmith. Further examples of the practice of wearing the helmet back to front, using the longer neck-shade as a peak, are evident in this photograph.

42. Skirmishers of the West Yorkshire Regiment in the attack on Monte Cristo, February 1900. Their field equipment comprises a loose haversack on the back above the roll carried at the rear of the waist, together with ammunition pouches and water canteen. The central figure has fastened his chinstrap around the rear peak of his helmet. The man at the extreme left has a khaki helmet with pagri flash on the side; the others appear to have khaki helmet covers.

43. Members of the 2nd Bn. the Dorsetshire Regiment attempting to recover shells dumped by the Boers in a pond near Ermelo. The central figure wears a dark 'jumper' and a knitted wool 'cap comforter'.

44. A skirmish line of the 2nd Bn. the Queen's Regiment, supposedly in action upon Buller's relief column for Ladysmith. The men are not, however, carrying full field equipment, and note the officers at the rear, including one who appears to be a conspicuous target!

45. Kit inspection, Blockhouse 27, 2nd Bn. West Yorkshire Regiment, 1902, showing the diversity of costume found even within the same platoon.

44▲ 45▼

▲46　▼47

46. A heliograph in use in the field at Dundee. The observer, reading signals from another party, has braced his telescope against his leg
47. Infantrymen, probably from the 2nd Bn. the Devonshire Regiment, relax in front of their tents along the Tugela. Note the woollen 'cap comforters' and the iron heel-plates on the boots.
48. The band of the 4th Bn. the Cameronians at Boshof. Three of the pipers wear 'doublets', which appear to be ordinary tunics with the skirts cut away to clear the sporran.
49. The 2nd Battalion, the Gordon Highlanders, escorting prisoners at Pietersburg The kilt was not suitable for South African servic (at Modder River the Argyll and Sutherland had their legs so sunburned that they appeared to have been sandpapered), but it was jealously retained by the Highlanders, with a khaki apron to aid camouflage which 'flapped up to such an extent as to be of little practical use'.

▲50

50. Members of the King's Own Scottish Borderers during the voyage to South Africa. All wear the diced glengarry, the uniforms being a mixture of dress doublets and khaki jackets. It was common aboard ship for soldiers to carry their clasp knife on a lanyard around the neck.

51. Boer artillery with guns captured after the destruction of the armoured train, 12 October 1899. The undress uniform of the ZAR *Staatsartillerie*, worn during the war, consisted of a light-coloured tunic and breeches ('mouse-coloured', fading to white), with a slouch hat looped at the right. The OVS artillery may have worn a greyish undress uniform with a darker collar and orange piping,

although their last field dress was a brownish-white single-breasted tunic with a standing collar for officers and a turn-down collar for other ranks, devoid of insignia.

52. Boer riflemen, including three in uniform, presumably the dress tunic of the ZAR *Staatsartillerie*. It is uncertain how widespread was the use of the blue tunic on active service, but some British accounts mention a blue uniform in use at the siege of Kimberley by the OVS artillery.

53. Boers in the trenches around Ladysmith, sheltering behind a rudimentary fortification made of piled rocks.

▼51

52▲   53▼

▲54   ▼55   ▼56

30

54. A Boer camp, showing a rudimentary field kitchen and a typical assortment of civilian clothing.

55. Schalk Burger, Vice-President of the Transvaal and Acting President after Kruger's flight. The bandolier and binocular case were often the sole equipment of Boer officers.

56. General Louis Botha. A contemporary British commentator remarked scathingly, 'He is fairly well educated for a Boer, and talks English fluently when he pleases'. Viewing the war as an unmitigated disaster, he was a capable leader and became South Africa's first Prime Minister. He wears a typical 'service uniform' for the period.

57. Commandant Koos De la Rey, 'a striking model for some warrior prophet of the Old Testament'. Perhaps the most innovative commander of the war, he was a very chivalrous opponent, as demonstrated by his dealings with the wounded Methuen whom he captured at Tweebosch. His equipment here is restricted to a binocular case and pistol belt; his horse-holder wears a waistcoat fitted with external ammunition pouches.

58. General Lukas Meyer, who commanded the Boers at Talana.

57▲   58▼

31

▲59

▲60 ▼61

**. Boer riflemen. Pur-
rting to show the
tion at Spion Kop, this
otograph is obviously
sed, as flags would not
 raised to mark the
sition of snipers! Both
en wear hat badges;
ckades of *Vierkleur*
our-colour) ribbons in
e Transvaal colours of
een, red, white and
ue pinned on the hat or
at were usually the
tent of Boer
niforms'.

. Boer ladies went out
n commando' like their
enfolk. This is Mrs.
tto Krantz, who fought
ongside her husband at
andslaagte, on the
ugela, and after.

. A Boer Armstrong
un and crew outside
adysmith; the man
cond from right
ppears to wear the
rlier pattern of OVS
taatsartillerie undress
niform, lightish grey
ith a darker collar and
oulder-straps.

2. The famous 'three
enerations' photo-
raph, shown here in
ne of its earliest pub-
shed versions. It
ypifies the unity of the
oer resistance.

3. Natal Carbineers in
eld dress. Note the
arksmanship badge on
e sleeve.

62▲   63▼

▲64
65▶

64. Officers of the Cape Volunteers. Like the striped pagri, the braided lanyard appears to be a regimental distinction. The officer on the right apparently carries the Royal Artillery variant of the 1822-pattern sword, instead of the cavalry sabre of the others.
65. Colonel William H. Mackinnon, City Imperial Volunteers. An ex-Guards and staff officer, William Mackinnon commanded the

'CIVs', whose uniform is illustrated. Note the bronzed letters 'CIV' on the upturned brim of the hat. The 1895-pattern sword has a khaki fabric cover over the guard, camouflaging the bright metal hilt; officers normally used the brown leather scabbard shown here though cavalry troopers on active service retained the steel hilt and scabbard on their swords, but both painted khaki-drab.

. Brig. Gen. Sir John G.
artnell. Aged 62 in 1900,
artnell was born in Ontario,
d served with distinction in
e Indian Mutiny and on the
rontier, and for almost thirty
ars had headed the Natal
ounted Police. A popular
ader, a great character and
e life and soul of the camp',
artnell gave De Wet a sharp
eck at Tigerkloof Sprint but
signed after Kitchener
fused his request for rein-
rcements shortly afterwards.
ote here the non-regulation
untlets and the lace-up black
ding boots.

. Officers and NCOs of the
atal Guides. Unusually, all
ear pith helmets instead of the
ore common slouch hat.

. Officers and sergeants of 'A'
quadron, South African Light
orse, a colonial corps formed
1899 with a leavening of
exans. Their insignia was a
lume of long, black tail-
athers of the Sakabula; the
ulu motto borne on their
altese cross badge was 'Usiba
jalo Nga Pambili', or
eathers at the Front'. At first
cknamed 'The Sakabulas',
ey were later called 'Cocky-
lie Birds'. The officer in the
ntre appears to be wearing
ricket flannels and boots.

◀66

67▲   68▼

69. A South African volunteer in typical campaign dress. Service in shirt-sleeves was commonplace, a comment concerning the operations before Colenso indicating the usual attitude to such unconventional dress: 'The Imperials and Thorneycroft's rode in shirt-sleeves, and it says something for the emancipation of modern British generals from the shackles of martinetism that the hardy rough-riders were allowed to dress in this fashion'

70. Lt. Smitherman of the Rhodesian Regiment, who penetrated the Boer lines into Mafeking and returned with reports to Plumer. He wears an unconventional though by no means unique costume.

71. Major F. R. Burnham of the Intelligence Staff, a Canadian skilled in the tracking and woodcraft of the North American Indians. In both the Matabele War and the Boer War he was invaluable as a scout.

72. Major D. P. Driscoll, an Irish settler in Burma, who volunteered to serve in South Africa as Gatacre's orderly. Later a captain in the Border Mounted Rifles, he formed his own corps of fifty scouts, with which he forced the surrender of Rouxville.

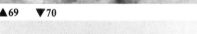

▲69　▼70　　　　▲71　▼72

73. 'Baden Powell's Police': four sergeant-majors on detached duty, originally serving with the 10th Hussars, Protectorate and Rhodesian regiments, and the 2nd Life Guards.

74. A group of Scottish irregulars who acted as scouts for the besieged Kimberley. Dressed typically for early Town Guard units, they have no uniform, though some such corps wore just a cockade with their civilian clothes; this was a return to the 'field-sign' of the seventeenth century (the Ladysmith corps, for example, wore dark red). Note the bagpipes!

73▲ 74▼

75. Baden Powell in his 'bush' uniform, including thick cloth leggings and pistol positioned for a cross-draw.

76. Officers of the Bechuanaland Rifles, a corps of five officers and 77 men which served with distinction through the siege of Mafeking: (left to right) Lts. Gemmell and McKenna; Capt. Cowan (commandant); Rev. H. Weekes (chaplain); and Lts. Minchin and Hayes (surgeon). Note the Maltese cross badge worn on Rev. Weekes' collar.

77. 'Baden Powell's Rough Riders': a muster of Rhodesian Irregular Horse, demonstrating a total lack of uniformity.

78. Lt. Bowers (centre) of the Cape Mounted Rifles, with his 'intelligence staff' of Col. Scobell's column, members of the CMR (with striped pagris) and white and coloured scouts. Neither side wanted to employ natives as combatants, in case they might turn upon the whites, but they served as watchmen and guards in tribal districts, and latterly as scouts who were armed for their own protection; this policy stiffened Boer resistance, the spectre of armed natives having haunted them for decades. The CMR's service uniform consisted of khaki drill with cord breeches, slouch hat and leather *Stohwasser* gaiters or blue puttees.

▲75 ▼76

▲79 ▼80

79. A camp of the staff of the Cape Cavalry Brigade during the pursuit of De Wet. Seated around the folding table and tea urn are Brig. Gen. Bethune (centre, wearing soft-topped cap), Col. J. Dunlop, chief of staff (left, wearing a civilian cloth cap) and Maj. Butcher, Brigade-Major (right, wearing forage-cap). *The Times* correspondent Lionel James is seated on the ground. Note the camp bed visible beneath the tent flap.

80. The Naval Brigade, drawn from Royal Navy ships, served with distinction in the Boer War. This unusual photograph shows Commander Morgan with Lts. James and Townsend of HMS *Tartar*, landed at Durban to impound the assets of the ZAR National Bank. Blue uniform is still in use, with interesting detail of officers' equipment harness, with and without blanket-roll.

81. Lt. Townsend of *Tartar* commanding his ship's landing-party at Durban, now wearing a khaki jacket, with shoulder-boards of rank, and a straw 'sennit' hat.

82. Capt. E. P. Jones and members of HMS *Forte*'s naval brigade. The men wear naval blouses in khaki, with the usual rank and trade insignia, and hat-bands lettered with the name of the ship.

81▲   82▼

▲83   ▼84

83. Medical staff of the Naval Brigade, including Fleet-Surgeon Porter. Note the ratings with khaki tunics and straw hats covered with khaki cloth; petty officers wore helmets. All are armed with revolvers and cutlasses, despite their Red Cross duties.

84. One of four 94pdr French Creusot guns bought by the Transvaal and used to bombard Mafeking. Nicknamed 'Creaky' or 'Big Ben' by the defenders, its first shell alarmed the garrison ('ladies wept and the men's faces blanched'), but its reputation was not justified by its effect: during the siege it fired 1,497 shells but killed fewer than twenty people.

85. Boer artillerymen. Note the handspike inserted in the gun's trail, used for traversing the weapon.

86. A 7pdr Krupp artillery piece used against Mafeking and captured at Johannesburg.

85▲ 86▼

▲87

87. One of HMS *Terrible*'s 4.7in guns firing at Colenso, at a target some 7,200yds distant. Note the distinctive carriage of these huge guns, and the unmistakable silhouette of the straw-hatted Naval Brigade crew.

88. A Vickers-Maxim 1pdr 'pom-pom' gun. The shells were fed in on a belt and continued to be fired as long as the trigger was depressed. Each shell fragmented into fifteen pieces upon bursting.

89. A heliograph (a signalling device for transmitting Morse code by a flashing mirror) photographed in Zululand, probably being operated by the Natal Mounted Police. A telescope with tripod is placed by the side of the man with a semaphore flag.

90. A Maxim gun detachment with a crew of infantrymen. The gun illustrated belongs to the 3rd Volunteer Battalion, Hampshire Regiment, who wear foreign service uniform.

▼88

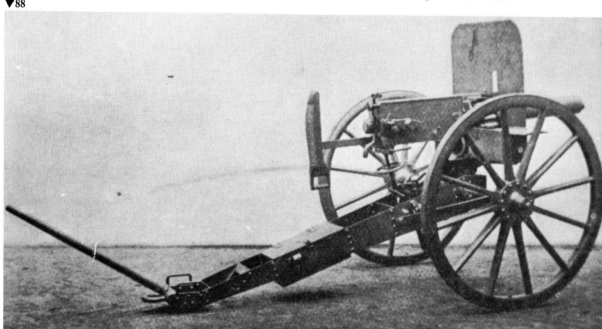

89▲   90▼

▲91　▼92

93▲

94▲

1. Members of Thorneycroft's Mounted Infantry, armed with Martinis. The photograph is interesting for the amount of ammunition carried by the men, who have shoulder-bandoliers and waist-pouches – a necessary requirement for operations conducted at some distance from the source of re-supply.
2. A provost platoon of General Douglas' column, assembled from the various units involved, the Loyal Regiment, the Northumberland and Munster Fusiliers and New Zealanders. The officers seated in the centre are, right, Provost-Marshal Capt. R. C. Boyle (Munsters) and, left, Lt. Matthews (New Zealand). This was quoted in 1901 as evidence of 'how Marvellously the Empire has Knitted Together by this War'.

93, 94. Walker's Maritzburg Hotchkiss gun detachment, a corps which served at Ladysmith, illustrating the deliberate faking of an ostensibly 'active service' photograph by changing the background from the public demonstration of the original.

▲95　　　　　　　　　　　▼96

95. A 'pom-pom' Maxim gun in action, showing the crew of four (one kneeling at the rear), with a 'spotter' with telescope in the background.
96. Lt.Col. St. L. Moore, 17th Bn. Imperial Yeomanry (including companies from the Leicestershire Yeomanry and Hampshire Carabiniers), photographed in service dress aboard the SS *Galeka* en route to South Africa.
97. An ammunition column on the march. Note especially the rolled greatcoats worn bandolier-fashion and the neck-protector at the rear of one helmet.
98. Field equipment of the Imperial Yeomanry. A comment of 1900 observes that '. . . the softer sex will think, as they look at the Imperial Yeoman in his field service kit, that in appearance he does not come up to the gallant Yeomanry Cavalry with whom they have been hitherto familiar, that brave figure in the green and gold jacket . . . when war becomes a stern reality even the feminine mind begins to appreciate the fact that the gilt and ginger-bread side of it must be turned to the wall . . .'

97▲   98▼

99. Officers of the 42nd Squadron, Imperial Yeomanry, raised in Norwich by the Loyal Suffolk Hussars, 1900. Seated the commanding officer, Capt. John R. Harvey. Each officer wears a different pattern of belt

100. Sergeants of Bethune's Mounted Infantry, wearing the widest possible variety of clothing, as befitted a unit renowned for its 'complete absence of red tapeism' (to quote one contemporary report).

101. A group of troopers and lance-corporals, believed to be from the Royal Wiltshire Yeomanry, which, as befitted the senior regiment of yeomanry, formed the first two companies of the 1st Battalion, the Imperial Yeomanry. Note the regimental Prince of Wales plumes badge worn over the chevrons.

102. A Mounted Infantryman with full field equipment, including a large net of forage and an eye-shade for the horse.

▲99   ▼100

101▲ 102▼

103, 104. Two more illustrations showing Imperial Yeomanry field equipment. Note, in photograph 103, the carbine carried in its bucket.
105. The 53rd Company, Imperial Yeomanry (East Kent), in typical field dress, with extra ammunition bandoliers and the slouch hat in a remarkable variety of guises.
106. The 25th Company, Imperial Yeomanry (West Somerset), photographed on their arrival home at Taunton in June 1901. Lt. Howell DSO stands in civilian clothes by the machine-gun.

▲103 ▼104

105▲   106▼

▲107 ▼108

107. Three members of the Honourable Artillery Company serving with the mounted section of the City Imperial Volunteers, the London volunteer corps raised in 1899 at the expense of commercial concerns and which served with distinction in the Boer War. The men are shown wearing khaki ordinary uniform, with leather gaiters instead of the puttees of the infantry detachment.

108. Members of the 6th Dragoon Guards at Arundel, loading machine-gun belts. Note the helmets worn back to front, with the neck-shade used as a sun vizor.

109. The red tunic worn in South Africa with khaki helmet and trousers, as shown in the officers' mess of the 3rd Bn. Durham Light Infantry (the old Durham Militia) at East London. This is an unusual spectacle, especially as the men have the brand-new 'Wolseley' helmet!

110. Capt. A. D. Fleming, 1st Volunteer Service Company, Royal Warwickshire Regiment, drawn from that regiment's 1st and 2nd Volunteer Battalions, which when first mustered wore the dark green 'rifle' uniform of the 1st VB and white tropical helmet.

111. Army Nursing Sister Clara Evans, from St. Helens, who died of dysentery at Bloemfontein. The Danish cross above the red cross on the brassard was bestowed by the Princess of Wales (later Queen Alexandra), who subsequently gave her name to the British Army's nursing corps. Nursing sisters on occasion accompanied the mobile field hospitals (though were not officially supposed to); Stationary Hospitals had four sisters each, and General Base Hospitals a minimum of twenty. In addition to the grey dresses with white accoutrements, the nurses' off-duty uniform included a straw boater with scarlet ribbon and a white parasol lined in scarlet.

109▲ 110▼ 111▼

▲112　▼113　　　　　　　▼114

112. Nursing staff of the Natal Volunteer Hospital, Pieter-maritzburg.

113. Sgt. W. S. Inder, from the Kendal Division of the St. John Ambulance Brigade, and bearer section of the 2nd Volunteer Battalion, Border Regiment. Inder described his uniform as being 'the colour of bath bricks', to which was added a blue stocking cap and fatigue cap, khaki helmet and a black-covered canteen; he was forced to change his original brass buttons to the regulation black, as shown here.

114. A volunteer of the Irish Hospital Corps; of especial note is the sleeve insignia, a red cross over 'IH'. The great length of the coat demonstrates a common problem: although this is a 'studio' portrait, the hem of the coat is plastered with mud!

115. Casualties are unloaded from an ambulance at the Portland Hospital. The stretcher-bearers are St. John personnel, wearing their curious khaki helmet, shaped like a police helmet instead of that worn by the army.

116. A Boer ambulance and medical staff.

115▲ 116▼

▲117

▲118　▼119

117. The slouch hat provided scope for a variety of colourful insignia, in the form of badges and coloured pagris, to be worn, as shown in this photograph of a corporal of Montmorency's Scouts. One of the most flamboyant hat designs, it features a plume and two badges, a side-patch inscribed 'Scout', and a skull and crossed bones on the front, apparently copied from the 17th Lancers.

118. The hat badge of the City Imperial Volunteers was the letters 'CIV' in black or bronze. Shown here is Lt. W. L. B. Alt, aged 22, the first CIV officer to be killed in the war, near Pretoria in June 1900.

119. Capt. E. D. Chittenden, adjutant of the Prince of Wales' Light Horse, formed of Welshmen resident in Cape Town. In addition to the coloured pagri, the brim bears badges of the Prince of Wales' plumes over a Welsh dragon (other photographs show the plumes worn alone).

120. Simon, 16th Lord Lovat, in the uniform of his Lovat Scouts, a corps of Scottish ghillies adept in tracking and fieldcraft. They wore a khaki tunic with four pockets and a khaki cloth belt, and a slouch hat with khaki pagri and a piece of tartan on the brim, believed to have been 'Red Fraser'.

121. Officers of the Imperial Corps of Guides at an impromptu camp. Though of poor quality, this privately taken photograph shows the hat decorations (including a huge rosette, extreme right) of Col. M. F. Rimington's intelligence corps, formed from loyal South African farmers and nicknamed 'Rimington's Tigers', from the leopardskin pagri and wildcat tails worn on their hats.

122. Members of the City Imperial Volunteers peeling potatoes at a bivouac on the veldt. The 'CIV' badge is just visible on the brim of the hat worn by the figure seated on the extreme right; the standing figure appears to have manufactured a rudimentary sun shade by wearing a handkerchief over his head, underneath his hat.

▼120

121▲   122▼

123. Colonel Thorneycroft and another officer. Especially notable is the regimental pagri flash on the 'Wolseley' helmet, 'TMI' (for 'Thorneycroft's Mounted Infantry').

124. Major Jowsey of the New Zealand Rough Riders. New Zealand was the first colony to offer troops for service in South Africa. They were 'mostly tall, athletic, and strong in wind and limb. Hardship does not easily tell upon them . . . a quality they share with most of the Colonial troops – men bred in the country oftener than in the town', according to a contemporary report.

125. Volunteers from Canada: three members of the North-West Mounted Police who served in South Africa, seen here with their distinctive hats.

▲123 ▼124

125▶

126. Private James Kennedy of the Canadian contingent. Apart from the interest in the uniform (note the narrow-brimmed hat and low collar), this photograph is noteworthy in demonstrating the resilience of the human body. Kennedy was shot eleven times but survived, though he was thenceforth burdened with the nickname 'The Human Sieve'!

127. Australian volunteers of the Imperial Bushmen, a corps of irregular horse, wearing a distinctive costume of short jackets and soft khaki caps.

128. Trooper John H. Bisdee of the Tasmanian Imperial Bushmen, one of the first two Australians to win the Victoria Cross whilst serving with an Australian unit under British command, at Warm Bad, Transvaal, in September 1900. He wears full field equipment in this photograph; note the picket-rope and horseshoe case carried by the saddle.

129. Numerous foreign volunteers offered to help the Boers, both idealists and soldiers of fortune. They were received coolly, Kruger remarking to some Germans, 'Thank you for coming. Don't imagine that we had need of you. Transvaal wants no foreign help but as you wish to fight for us you are welcome'. Many went home immediately! This photograph shows American volunteers, with a small US flag; included in the group is Webster Davis, formerly Assistant Secretary of the US Department of the Interior, who spent some time with the Boers and then returned to the United States to participate in pro-Boer agitation.

126 ▶

▼127

130. Blake's Irish Brigade, an Irish-American nationalist corps commanded by Col. John Y. F. Blake, West Pointer who had helped capture Geronimo. The 'brigade' was reinforced by the 'Chicago Irish American Ambulance Corps' raised by a militant Irish-American society, Clan-na-Gael, and wore US Army clothing, discarding its Red Cross insignia once it had arrived in South Africa. Never more than 180 strong, the Irish corps offended many principled Boers by their profanity and drinking, and were discharged in autumn 1900 as being of little use in the guerrilla war.

131. Boers with captured British equipment. The standing figure in the centre carries a Lee-Metford rifle with bayonet, whilst the standing figure on the right wears the 1888-pattern Slade-Wallace cartridge pouches.

132. Military attachés with Lord Roberts, showing a diversity of tropical uniforms worn by the great powers. Standing are Maj. Gentilini (Italy) and Capt. Luttwitz (Germany); seated are Capt. d'Amade (France) and Col. Stakevich (Russia); and squatting are Capt. Slocum (USA) and Col. Trimmel (Austria).

132

▲130   ▼131

▲ 133

133. Private Jack of the 1st Volunteer Battalion, Royal Warwickshire Regiment, who deserted from the Boers and was enlisted as a member of the Warwickshire's Volunteer Service Company. Veteran of all their engagements, he was smuggled home, given a uniform jacket, presented with his campaign medal by General Sir Reginald Pole-Carew, and granted an annuity to keep him in biscuits, becoming 'the best-known dog in Birmingham'.

▲ 134

134. The end of the war. This photograph is believed to show a Boer prisoner and his British guard, who wears the black mourning brassard for the death of Queen Victoria.

135. Casualties of Colenso and Spion Kop, this group of invalids is pictured having landed from their transport after being evacuated home. A variety of uniforms is visible, including a couple featuring the white helmet with khaki covers removed.

▼ 135